Morgan Donovan

How To Monetize Your TikTok Account.

A Complete Guide to Monetizing Your Creative Journey On TikTok

Copyright © 2024 by Morgan Donovan

All rights reserved. No part of this publication may be reproduced, stored or transmitted in any form or by any means, electronic, mechanical, photocopying, recording, scanning, or otherwise without written permission from the publisher. It is illegal to copy this book, post it to a website, or distribute it by any other means without permission.

First edition

This book was professionally typeset on Reedsy
Find out more at *reedsy.com*

"Creativity is contagious. Pass it on." - Albert Einstein

Morgan Donovan

Contents

Foreword 1
Preface 4
1. The Rise of TikTok...7
2. Building Your Brand 11
3. Growing Your Audience 14
4. Engaging Your Community.............................18
5. Monetization Strategies 21
6. Building a Sustainable Income 25
7. Legal and Financial Considerations 29
8. Overcoming Challenges 33
9. Case Studies and Success Stories 36
10. Looking to the Future 40
11. Conclusion: Embrace the Journey 44
    1.
    2.
    3.
    4.
    5.
    6.
    7.
    8.

9.
10.
11.
12.

Foreword

Foreword

In today's fast-paced digital landscape, TikTok has emerged as a powerhouse platform, captivating millions with its short-form videos and fostering a community of creators unlike any other. From viral dance trends to heartfelt storytelling, TikTok offers a canvas for creativity where imagination knows no bounds.

In "How To Monetize Your TikTok Account: A Complete Guide to Monetizing Your Creative Journey On TikTok," you're about to embark on an exhilarating journey into the world of content creation, entrepreneurship, and self-expression. As the digital landscape continues to evolve, TikTok presents unprecedented opportunities for individuals to turn their passions into profits, their hobbies into hustles, and their dreams into reality.

This guide is not just a roadmap to financial success; it's a manifesto for the creative soul. It's a testament to the power of authenticity, resilience, and determination in a world saturated with content and competition. Through practical advice, insightful anecdotes, and actionable strategies, you'll learn how to navigate the complexities of the TikTok ecosystem, seize opportunities for monetization, and carve out your own unique path to success.

But more than that, this guide is a celebration of the human spirit – of the dreamers, the doers, and the disruptors who dare to defy the status quo and forge their own destiny. It's a reminder that no matter where you come from or what obstacles you face, your voice matters, your story is valid, and your potential is limitless.

So as you dive into the pages ahead, I encourage you to approach this journey with an open mind, a courageous heart, and an unwavering commitment to your vision. Whether you're a seasoned creator or just starting out, remember that every challenge is an opportunity, every setback is a lesson, and every success is a testament to your resilience and tenacity.

Embrace the journey, trust in your instincts, and above all, believe in yourself. The world is waiting for your voice, your talent, and your unique perspective. So let's make some magic, ignite some dreams, and monetize our TikTok accounts one inspired video at a time.

Here's to your creative journey and the boundless possibilities that lie ahead. Let's make history, one TikTok at a time.

Warm regards,

[Morgan   Donovan]

Preface

Preface

Welcome to "How To Monetize Your TikTok Account: A Complete Guide to Monetizing Your Creative Journey On TikTok." by Morgan Donovan

In today's digital age, social media platforms like TikTok have revolutionized the way we connect, create, and consume content. With its vibrant community, innovative features, and unparalleled reach, TikTok has become a playground for creativity, where individuals from around the world can share their talents, passions, and stories with the click of a button.

But TikTok is more than just a platform for entertainment; it's also a gateway to opportunity. With the rise of influencer marketing, brand partnerships, and creator funds, TikTok creators have the potential to turn their passion for content creation into a lucrative career. Whether you're a dancer, comedian, chef, artist, or entrepreneur, there are endless possibilities for monetizing your TikTok account and building a sustainable income stream from your creative endeavors.

In this comprehensive guide, we'll explore the strategies, techniques, and best practices for monetizing your TikTok account and maximizing your earning potential as a content creator. From understanding TikTok's algorithm and building your brand to growing your audience, negotiating sponsorship deals, and navigating the legal and financial considerations of influencer marketing, this book covers everything you need to know to succeed in the competitive world of TikTok.

But beyond the practical advice and actionable tips, this guide is also a celebration of creativity, authenticity, and passion. It's a reminder that success on TikTok – and in life – is not just about the numbers or the accolades, but about the journey, the growth, and the impact you make along the way.

So whether you're just starting out on TikTok or looking to take your content to the next level, I invite you to join me on this creative journey. Let's unlock the full potential of your TikTok account, turn your passion into profit, and make your mark on the world one video at a time.

Get ready to monetize your TikTok account and embark on the adventure of a lifetime. Your creative journey starts now.

Yours truly,
    Morgan   Donovan

1

The Rise of TikTok

The Rise of TikTok

Introduction:

In the vast universe of social media platforms, one app has risen above the rest, capturing the hearts and minds of millions worldwide: TikTok. Born from the merger of Musical.ly and Douyin, TikTok burst onto the scene in 2016, quickly becoming a global sensation. Its meteoric rise is a testament to the power of innovation and the insatiable appetite for creative expression in the digital age.

Understanding TikTok's Explosive Growth:

TikTok's ascent to prominence can be attributed to several key factors. Its intuitive interface, seamless editing tools, and addictive algorithm have transformed the way we consume and create content. Unlike its predecessors, TikTok thrives on short-form video content, catering to the ever-dwindling attention spans of its users. Its algorithm, fueled by machine learning, analyzes user behavior to deliver a personalized feed of content tailored to individual preferences, ensuring maximum engagement and retention.

The Power of Virality:

At the heart of TikTok's success lies the power of virality. A single video, cleverly crafted and perfectly timed, has the potential to reach millions overnight, catapulting its creator to internet stardom. Whether it's a catchy dance routine, a hilarious skit, or a heartwarming moment, TikTok thrives on content that elicits an emotional response and encourages users to share with their friends and followers.

Exploring the Diverse Range of Content:

One of the most remarkable aspects of TikTok is its sheer diversity of content. From comedy sketches to cooking tutorials, dance challenges to DIY hacks, there's something for everyone on the platform. Whether you're a budding chef, an aspiring musician, or a fashion enthusiast, TikTok offers a platform to showcase your talents and connect with like-minded individuals around the world.

Identifying Your Niche:

In a sea of endless possibilities, finding your niche on TikTok is essential to standing out from the crowd. Take the time to explore different genres and styles of content, paying close attention to what resonates with you and your audience. Are you passionate about fitness, beauty, or gaming? Do you have a unique talent or perspective to share? By identifying your niche early on, you can focus your efforts on creating content that aligns with your interests and expertise, setting the stage for success in the competitive world of TikTok.

Teaching:

Aspiring TikTok creators often overlook one of the platform's most powerful features: its potential as a teaching tool. Whether you're sharing life hacks, offering language lessons, or providing academic tutorials, TikTok provides a platform to educate and inspire others in creative ways. By leveraging your expertise and passion for teaching, you can establish yourself as a trusted authority in your niche, attracting followers who value your knowledge and insight.

2

Building Your Brand

Building Your Brand

Crafting a Compelling Profile:

Your TikTok profile serves as your digital calling card, offering a glimpse into who you are and what you stand for. To make a lasting impression, it's essential to craft a profile that reflects your personality and interests. Choose a profile picture that captures your essence and a username that is memorable and easy to find. Write a catchy bio that highlights your passions, expertise, and what sets you apart from the crowd. Remember, your profile is the first impression you make on potential followers, so make it count.

Developing a Content Strategy:

Behind every successful TikTok account lies a well-thought-out content strategy. Before diving into content creation, take the time to define your goals and target audience. What kind of content do you want to create? Who are you trying to reach? Once you have a clear understanding of your objectives, brainstorm ideas for content that resonates with your audience's interests and preferences. Whether it's entertaining skits, informative tutorials, or heartfelt storytelling, your content should reflect your unique voice and perspective. Consistency is key, so establish a posting schedule and stick to it to keep your audience engaged and coming back for more.

Leveraging Trends and Challenges:

TikTok is a platform fueled by trends and challenges, offering endless opportunities to tap into the collective creativity of its users. Keep an eye on the latest trends and challenges circulating on the platform and find creative ways to incorporate them into your content. Whether it's putting your own spin on a popular dance challenge or participating in a viral hashtag challenge, leveraging trends can help increase your visibility and engagement. However, authenticity is crucial, so be sure to stay true to your brand and values while participating in trends and challenges.

Teaching:

Incorporating educational content into your TikTok strategy can help you stand out from the crowd and establish yourself as a trusted authority in your niche. Whether you're sharing life hacks, offering advice, or providing tutorials, teaching content has the power to inform, inspire, and entertain your audience. When creating educational content, focus on providing value and solving problems for your audience. Keep your explanations clear and concise, and use visual aids and examples to enhance understanding. By positioning yourself as a teacher and mentor, you can attract followers who are eager to learn from your expertise and insights.

The importance of building your brand on TikTok, including crafting a compelling profile, developing a content strategy, and leveraging trends and challenges to increase visibility and engagement, focusing on these key elements, you can lay the foundation for a successful TikTok presence and establish yourself as a leader in your niche.

3

Growing Your Audience

Growing Your Audience

Techniques for Attracting Followers Organically:

Building a loyal and engaged following on TikTok requires more than just posting content; it requires a strategic approach to attracting followers organically. Start by optimizing your content for discovery by using relevant keywords, captions, and hashtags. Engage with your audience by responding to comments, liking and sharing other users' content, and participating in duets and challenges. Consistency is key, so establish a regular posting schedule and stick to it to keep your audience engaged and coming back for more. Lastly, don't underestimate the power of authenticity; be genuine, relatable, and true to yourself, and your audience will naturally gravitate towards you.

Collaborating with Other TikTok Creators:

Collaboration is a powerful way to expand your reach and grow your audience on TikTok. Partnering with other creators allows you to tap into their existing fanbase and introduce your content to a new audience. Look for creators who share similar interests or target demographics and reach out to them to propose collaboration ideas. Whether it's a duet, a joint challenge, or a cross-promotional shoutout, collaborating with other TikTok creators can help you reach new followers and build valuable connections within the community.

Utilizing Hashtags and Cross-Promotion:

Hashtags are a vital tool for increasing your discoverability and reaching a wider audience on TikTok. Research popular and relevant hashtags in your niche and incorporate them into your content to increase its visibility. Don't just stick to generic hashtags; experiment with niche and trending hashtags to maximize your reach. Additionally, consider cross-promoting your TikTok content on other social media platforms such as Instagram, Twitter, and Facebook. Share teasers, behind-the-scenes footage, or highlights from your TikTok videos to drive traffic to your TikTok profile and attract new followers.

Teaching:

Teaching your audience about the strategies and techniques you use to grow your TikTok following can be a valuable way to engage with your community and establish yourself as a thought leader in your niche. Share tips, tricks, and best practices for attracting followers organically, collaborating with other creators, and utilizing hashtags and cross-promotion. Break down complex concepts into easy-to-understand explanations, and provide actionable advice that your audience can implement to grow their own TikTok presence. By sharing your knowledge and expertise, you not only provide value to your audience but also strengthen your relationship with them and foster a sense of trust and loyalty.

Explore techniques for growing your audience on TikTok, including attracting followers organically, collaborating with other creators, and utilizing hashtags and cross-promotion, implementing these strategies and sharing your knowledge with your audience, you can increase your visibility, expand your reach, and build a thriving community of followers on TikTok.

4

Engaging Your Community

Engaging Your Community

Fostering Genuine Connections:

Building a strong and loyal community on TikTok goes beyond just amassing followers; it requires fostering genuine connections with your audience. Take the time to engage with your followers by responding to comments, acknowledging their feedback, and addressing their questions and concerns. Show appreciation for their support by liking and sharing user-generated content featuring your brand. By actively engaging with your audience, you not only strengthen your relationship with them but also demonstrate that you value their input and contributions.

Hosting Live Streams and Q&A Sessions:

Live streaming is a powerful tool for engaging with your audience in real-time and fostering a sense of intimacy and connection. Host live streams on a regular basis to interact with your followers, answer their questions, and provide behind-the-scenes glimpses into your life and creative process. Consider hosting themed live streams or Q&A sessions focused on topics relevant to your niche to attract and retain viewers. Encourage audience participation by inviting them to ask questions, share their thoughts, and participate in interactive polls and challenges. By hosting live streams and Q&A sessions, you create opportunities for meaningful engagement and dialogue with your community, strengthening their loyalty and investment in your brand.

Incorporating User-Generated Content:

User-generated content (UGC) is a powerful tool for fostering a sense of community and belonging among your followers. Encourage your audience to create and share content featuring your brand, products, or hashtag to be featured on your profile or in your videos. Showcase user-generated content in your feed, stories, or highlights to highlight and celebrate your community's creativity and contributions. Consider running contests, challenges, or shoutout campaigns to incentivize user-generated content creation and encourage participation. By incorporating user-generated content into your content strategy, you not only showcase your community's talent and enthusiasm but also create opportunities for collaboration and co-creation, strengthening the bond between you and your followers.

Explanation:

Strategies for engaging your community on TikTok, including fostering genuine connections through comments and direct messages, hosting live streams and Q&A sessions to interact in real-time, and incorporating user-generated content to foster a sense of community, implementing these strategies, you can create a vibrant and engaged community of followers who are invested in your brand and eager to participate in your content creation journey.

5

Monetization Strategies

Monetization Strategies

Exploring Various Monetization Methods:

Monetizing your TikTok account opens up a world of opportunities to turn your passion for content creation into a lucrative income stream. One of the most common monetization methods is through brand partnerships, where you collaborate with brands to create sponsored content that promotes their products or services. Affiliate marketing is another popular option, where you earn a commission for promoting products or services and driving sales through affiliate links. Additionally, you can explore selling merchandise or digital products, such as e-books, courses, or exclusive content, to your followers. By diversifying your monetization methods, you can maximize your earning potential and build a sustainable income stream from your TikTok account.

Understanding TikTok's Creator Fund:

TikTok's Creator Fund provides an additional avenue for creators to monetize their content and earn money directly from the platform. The Creator Fund allows eligible creators to earn money based on the performance of their content, including views, engagement, and watch time. To qualify for the Creator Fund, creators must meet certain eligibility criteria, including having at least 100,000 followers, being at least 18 years old, and meeting minimum engagement thresholds. Once accepted into the Creator Fund, creators can earn money based on the performance of their content, with payments distributed on a monthly basis. Understanding the eligibility requirements and how the Creator Fund works can help you leverage this monetization option to supplement your income as a TikTok creator.

Negotiating Sponsorship Deals and Setting Rates:

As your TikTok account grows in popularity, you may have the opportunity to negotiate sponsorship deals with brands looking to reach your audience. When negotiating sponsorship deals, it's important to consider factors such as your audience demographics, engagement metrics, and the value you can offer to the brand. Take the time to research the brand and understand their goals and objectives for the partnership. Clearly communicate your value proposition and the benefits of partnering with you, including your reach, influence, and ability to drive engagement and conversions. When setting your rates as an influencer, consider factors such as your time, effort, and expertise, as well as industry benchmarks and your unique value proposition. By negotiating sponsorship deals and setting your rates strategically, you can ensure that you're compensated fairly for your work and expertise as a TikTok influencer.

Teaching:

Teaching others about the various monetization strategies available on TikTok empowers them to leverage their creativity and build a sustainable income stream from their content. By sharing insights, tips, and best practices for exploring brand partnerships, affiliate marketing, merchandise sales, and the TikTok Creator Fund, you can help aspiring creators navigate the monetization landscape and make informed decisions about their content strategy.

Teaching creators how to negotiate sponsorship deals and set their rates as influencers equips them with the knowledge and skills they need to advocate for themselves and maximize their earning potential on TikTok.

Sharing your expertise and insights can help others unlock the full potential of their TikTok accounts and achieve financial success as content creators.

Monetization strategies for TikTok creators, including brand partnerships, affiliate marketing, merchandise sales, and the TikTok Creator Fund,understanding these monetization methods and teaching others how to leverage them effectively, you can build a sustainable income stream from your TikTok account and turn your passion for content creation into a rewarding career.

6

Building a Sustainable Income

Building a Sustainable Income

Diversifying Your Revenue Streams:

As a TikTok creator, it's essential to diversify your income streams to ensure long-term financial stability. While brand partnerships and sponsorships can be lucrative, they can also be unpredictable. By exploring additional monetization methods such as affiliate marketing, merchandise sales, or digital product creation, you can spread your income across multiple streams, reducing reliance on any single source. This diversification not only provides stability but also opens up new opportunities for revenue generation, allowing you to weather any fluctuations in the market.

Creating Premium Content for Subscription-Based Platforms:

Subscription-based platforms like OnlyFans or Patreon offer TikTok creators a platform to monetize their content through premium subscriptions.

Offering exclusive content, behind-the-scenes access, or personalized perks to subscribers, you can cultivate a dedicated community of supporters and create a steady stream of recurring revenue. Consider what unique value you can offer to your subscribers and how you can differentiate your premium content from what you share on TikTok for free.

Providing additional value and incentives for subscribers, you can attract and retain loyal fans who are willing to pay for exclusive access to your content, ensuring a sustainable income over time.

Investing in Your Personal Brand:

Building a sustainable income as a TikTok creator requires more than just creating content; it requires investing in your personal brand and professional development. Take the time to refine your brand identity, including your unique voice, aesthetic, and values. Consider how you can differentiate yourself from other creators in your niche and position yourself as a trusted authority and influencer. Invest in professional development opportunities such as workshops, courses, or coaching to hone your skills and expand your knowledge base. Additionally, prioritize networking and building relationships within the industry to open up new opportunities for collaboration, mentorship, and growth. By investing in your personal brand and professional development, you can build a strong foundation for long-term success and sustainability as a TikTok creator, ensuring that you remain relevant and competitive in the ever-evolving landscape of social media.

Teaching:

Empowering others to build a sustainable income as TikTok creators is essential for the growth and sustainability of the creator community. By sharing insights, tips, and best practices for diversifying income streams, creating premium content, and investing in personal branding and professional development, you can help aspiring creators navigate the challenges of monetization and build successful and sustainable careers on TikTok. By teaching others how to diversify their revenue streams, create premium content, and invest in their personal brand, you contribute to the overall health and prosperity of the TikTok creator ecosystem, ensuring that creators have the knowledge and resources they need to thrive in the competitive world of social media.

Strategies for building a sustainable income as a TikTok creator, including diversifying revenue streams, creating premium content for subscription-based platforms, and investing in personal branding and professional development, implementing these strategies and teaching others how to do the same, you can build a thriving and sustainable career as a TikTok creator and achieve long-term financial success.

7

Legal and Financial Considerations

Legal and Financial Considerations

Navigating the Legal Landscape:

As a TikTok creator, it's crucial to navigate the legal landscape of influencer marketing to ensure compliance with regulations and protect yourself from potential legal issues. This includes adhering to Federal Trade Commission (FTC) guidelines, which require influencers to disclose any sponsored content or material connections with brands to their audience. Failure to disclose sponsorships can result in fines and damage to your reputation. Additionally, understanding copyright laws is essential to avoid infringing on the intellectual property rights of others. Always obtain proper permissions or licenses before using copyrighted material in your content, and be mindful of fair use guidelines when incorporating third-party content.

Setting Up a Business Entity:

Setting up a business entity, such as a sole proprietorship, partnership, LLC, or corporation, can offer legal protection and tax benefits for TikTok creators. By establishing a separate legal entity for your business, you can shield your personal assets from liability and protect yourself in the event of legal disputes or lawsuits. Additionally, operating as a business entity allows you to take advantage of tax deductions and incentives available to businesses, potentially lowering your tax burden and increasing your profitability. Consult with a legal or financial professional to determine the best business structure for your needs and ensure compliance with state and local regulations.

Managing Your Finances:

Managing your finances as a TikTok creator involves keeping accurate records of your income and expenses, budgeting effectively, and planning for taxes. Track your earnings from brand partnerships, sponsorships, affiliate marketing, merchandise sales, and other revenue streams, and keep receipts for any business-related expenses, such as equipment, supplies, or advertising costs. Set aside a portion of your income for taxes, as you may be responsible for self-employment taxes, income taxes, and other tax obligations. Consider working with an accountant or financial advisor to develop a financial plan and strategy for managing your finances effectively and ensuring long-term financial stability.

Seeking Professional Advice:

Seeking advice from professionals such as lawyers and accountants is essential for TikTok creators to ensure compliance with legal and financial regulations and protect themselves from potential liabilities. A lawyer can provide guidance on navigating the legal landscape of influencer marketing, drafting contracts, and protecting your intellectual property rights. An accountant can help you set up your business entity, manage your finances, and navigate tax obligations. Additionally, consider consulting with other professionals such as social media managers, branding experts, or insurance agents to address specific needs or concerns related to your TikTok career. By investing in professional advice and expertise, you can ensure compliance, mitigate risks, and achieve financial stability as a TikTok creator.

Legal and financial considerations for TikTok creators, including navigating the legal landscape of influencer marketing, setting up a business entity, managing finances, and seeking professional advice. Understanding and addressing these considerations, you can protect yourself from potential legal issues, manage your finances effectively, and build a successful and sustainable career as a TikTok creator.

8

Overcoming Challenges

Overcoming Challenges

Dealing with Burnout and Maintaining a Healthy Work-Life Balance:

As a TikTok creator, it's common to experience burnout due to the pressure to constantly create and engage with content. To overcome burnout and maintain a healthy work-life balance, prioritize self-care and set boundaries around your work. Schedule regular breaks, exercise, and relaxation activities to recharge and rejuvenate. Delegate tasks or seek support from friends, family, or collaborators to lighten your workload. Establish clear boundaries between work and personal life, and allocate dedicated time for both. Remember that your mental and physical well-being are paramount, and it's okay to take breaks and prioritize self-care when needed.

Handling Negative Feedback and Criticism with Resilience and Grace:

Receiving negative feedback and criticism is inevitable as a TikTok creator, but it's essential to handle it with resilience and grace. Instead of dwelling on negative comments or allowing them to affect your self-esteem, focus on constructive criticism and use it as an opportunity for growth and improvement. Respond to criticism with professionalism and maturity, acknowledging valid points and addressing concerns respectfully. Remember that not everyone will resonate with your content, and that's okay. Focus on creating content that aligns with your values and resonates with your true audience. Surround yourself with supportive friends, family, and fellow creators who uplift and encourage you during challenging times.

Continuously Evolving Your Content and Adapting to Changes in the TikTok Platform:

The TikTok platform is constantly evolving, with new trends, features, and algorithms shaping the content landscape. To stay relevant and successful as a TikTok creator, it's essential to continuously evolve your content and adapt to changes in the platform. Stay informed about the latest trends, challenges, and updates on TikTok, and experiment with new formats, styles, and techniques to keep your content fresh and engaging. Monitor your analytics and audience feedback to understand what resonates with your audience and adjust your content strategy accordingly. Embrace innovation and creativity, and don't be afraid to take risks and try new things. By staying agile and adaptable, you can thrive in the ever-changing world of TikTok and maintain a competitive edge as a creator.

Strategies for overcoming challenges as a TikTok creator, including dealing with burnout and maintaining a healthy work-life balance, handling negative feedback and criticism with resilience and grace, and continuously evolving your content and adapting to changes in the TikTok platform, implementing these strategies and prioritizing self-care, resilience, and innovation, you can overcome obstacles and achieve long-term success as a TikTok creator.

9

Case Studies and Success Stories

Case Studies and Success Stories

Examining Real-life Examples:

In this chapter, we'll delve into real-life examples of TikTok creators who have successfully monetized their accounts, turning their passion for content creation into profitable careers. We'll explore their strategies, mistakes, and triumphs to glean valuable insights and inspiration for our own journey as TikTok creators.

Case Study 1:

Meet Sarah, a fitness enthusiast and certified personal trainer who has amassed a loyal following on TikTok by sharing workout routines, nutrition tips, and motivational content. Sarah monetizes her TikTok account through a combination of brand partnerships, affiliate marketing, and merchandise sales. By collaborating with fitness brands, promoting workout supplements, and selling her own line of fitness apparel, Sarah has built a thriving business around her passion for health and fitness.

Case Study 2:

Next up, we have Jane, a fashion influencer and stylist who has cultivated a dedicated following on TikTok by sharing fashion hauls, styling tips, and trend forecasts. Jane monetizes her TikTok account through brand partnerships, sponsored content, and affiliate marketing. By collaborating with fashion brands, promoting clothing and accessories, and sharing affiliate links to her favorite products, Jane has turned her love for fashion into a profitable career as a TikTok creator.

Case Study 3:

Last but not least, we have Alex, a DIY enthusiast and creative genius who has built a massive following on TikTok by sharing do-it-yourself projects, crafting tutorials, and home decor ideas. Alex monetizes his TikTok account through brand partnerships, sponsored content, and digital product sales. By partnering with DIY brands, showcasing sponsored products, and selling digital guides and templates, Alex has transformed his passion for creativity into a lucrative income stream on TikTok.

Learning from Their Strategies, Mistakes, and Triumphs:

By examining the strategies, mistakes, and triumphs of successful TikTok creators like Sarah, Jane, and Alex, we can glean valuable insights and lessons to apply to our own journey as TikTok creators. From their innovative content ideas and strategic partnerships to their resilience in the face of challenges and setbacks, these creators offer a wealth of knowledge and inspiration for aspiring TikTok creators. By learning from their experiences and adapting their strategies to our own unique circumstances, we can overcome obstacles, capitalize on opportunities, and achieve our goals of monetizing our TikTok accounts and building successful careers as content creators.

Real-life case studies and success stories of TikTok creators who have successfully monetized their accounts. By examining their strategies, mistakes, and triumphs, we can gain valuable insights and inspiration to apply to our own journey as TikTok creators, helping us navigate the challenges and opportunities of the ever-evolving world of social media.

10

Looking to the Future

Looking to the Future

Speculating on the Future of TikTok and Social Media:

As we look to the future, the evolution of TikTok and the broader landscape of social media is sure to continue. With advancements in technology, changes in user behavior, and shifts in cultural trends, the possibilities for innovation and growth are endless. We can expect TikTok to continue expanding its features and offerings, introducing new tools for creators, and exploring opportunities for monetization and community-building. Additionally, we may see new platforms emerge, challenging the dominance of established players and pushing the boundaries of creativity and engagement. As TikTok creators, it's essential to stay agile and adaptable, embracing change and innovation as we navigate the ever-evolving landscape of social media.

Setting Long-term Goals and Aspirations:

As we chart our course for the future, it's important to set long-term goals and aspirations for our career as content creators. Whether it's reaching a certain number of followers, securing brand partnerships with our dream companies, or launching our own line of products or services, having clear goals helps us stay focused and motivated on our journey. Take the time to define your vision for success and break it down into actionable steps and milestones. Set SMART goals

(Specific, Measurable, Achievable, Relevant, Time-bound) and regularly assess your progress to ensure you're on track to achieving your long-term aspirations as a TikTok creator.

Embracing Creativity, Authenticity, and Passion:

As we look to the future, one thing remains constant: the importance of creativity, authenticity, and passion in sustaining success on TikTok and beyond. In a crowded and competitive landscape, it's our unique voice, perspective, and creativity that set us apart and resonate with our audience. Embrace your creativity, experiment with new ideas and formats, and stay true to yourself and your values. Authenticity is key to building genuine connections with your audience, so don't be afraid to show your personality, vulnerabilities, and imperfections. Finally, let your passion for content creation be your guiding light, fueling your drive, determination, and resilience in the face of challenges and setbacks. By embracing creativity, authenticity, and passion, we can cultivate a sustainable and fulfilling career as TikTok creators, inspiring and empowering others along the way.

We've speculated on the future of TikTok and the evolving landscape of social media, set long-term goals and aspirations for our career as content creators, and embraced creativity, authenticity, and passion as the keys to sustained success on TikTok and beyond. As we continue our journey as TikTok creators, let's remain open to change, committed to growth, and unwavering in our pursuit of excellence, knowing that the possibilities for success are limitless when we lead with creativity, authenticity, and passion.

11

Conclusion: Embrace the Journey

Conclusion: Embrace the Journey

As we reach the end of this journey, it's clear that TikTok has transformed the landscape of social media, offering unparalleled opportunities for creative expression, connection, and financial independence. What started as a platform for sharing short videos has evolved into a global phenomenon, empowering individuals from all walks of life to share their stories, showcase their talents, and build thriving communities.

Throughout this book, we've explored the various ways to monetize your TikTok account, from brand partnerships and affiliate marketing to merchandise sales and subscription-based platforms. We've learned about the importance of building a strong personal brand, engaging with your audience, and navigating the legal and financial considerations of being a TikTok creator.

But beyond the strategies and techniques, the heart of TikTok lies in its ability to amplify voices, spark creativity, and foster connections. It's a platform where authenticity reigns supreme, where anyone with a smartphone and a story to tell can find their voice and make an impact.

As you embark on your own TikTok journey, I encourage you to embrace your unique voice and perspective. Your authenticity is your greatest asset, and it's what will set you apart in a sea of content. Be fearless in sharing your truth, your passions, and your creativity with the world.

But remember, success on TikTok – and in life – is not just about the numbers or the accolades. It's about the journey, the growth, and the impact you make along the way. Embrace the ups and downs, the challenges and triumphs, knowing that each step forward brings you closer to your dreams.

So, to all the aspiring TikTok creators out there, I encourage you to pursue your dreams with determination and resilience. Believe in yourself, trust in your vision, and never be afraid to take that leap of faith. Your journey as a TikTok creator is just beginning, and the possibilities are endless. Embrace it, cherish it, and above all, enjoy the ride.

Here's to the transformative power of TikTok, and to the limitless potential of creators like you. Embrace the journey, and let your creativity shine.

The world is waiting.

All Rights Reserved
Morgan Donovan
2024

www.ingramcontent.com/pod-product-compliance
Lightning Source LLC
Chambersburg PA
CBHW050244230526
45470CB00005B/2108